# JOHNNY
## Catching Fire

AARON ALLEN

To order additional copies of this book, contact:
Xlibris
844-714-8691
www.Xlibris.com
Orders@Xlibris.com

KJV
Scripture quotations marked KJV are from the Holy
Bible, King James Version (Authorized Version).
First published in 1611. Quoted from the KJV Classic
Reference Bible, Copyright © 1983 by The Zondervan
Corporation.

ISBN:   Softcover        978-1-6641-3954-1
        Hardcover        978-1-6641-3953-4
        EBook            978-1-6641-3952-7


Print information available on the last page

Rev. date: 10/27/2020

# Contents

# I.

Johnny was walking home from school when he was met by his nemesis. Brock was the student everyone wanted to be like. Athletic and good looking—at least that's what all the girls were saying—Brock had made it his life's ambition to make Johnny's miserable. This day was no different.

"Hey, Johnny," he called. "Where'd you get that shirt? From a 1950s Salvation Army store?"

Actually, Brock was not that far-off. Since his father died, Johnny's mother had turned to purchasing his and his sister's clothes from garage sales and the local Salvation Army to make ends meet.

Johnny stopped to face his adversary. "None of your business, Brock! Leave me alone. You know what Principal Jim told you about staying away from me."

Principal Jim was tough but fair and had taken a liking to Johnny. Consciously or subconsciously, Johnny gravitated toward Principal Jim as a type of surrogate father and looked for every opportunity to visit his office. In fact, on one occasion, Johnny decided to visit with him on his lunch break. When Principal Jim asked Johnny what he could do for him, he responded, "Oh, nothing in particular. I just thought you might like some company." This only increased Principal Jim's affinity toward him.

Brock paid no attention to what Johnny said and, in a single motion, pushed him to the ground. The rage in Johnny bristled. If he were able, he would get up and pummel Brock. But he knew this would be a huge mistake. Brock was twice his size and, no doubt, twice as strong. So he just lay there, hoping Brock would see him as a waste of time and go his merry way. Fortunately, this is what happened, and a few minutes later, Johnny found his way home.

This night Johnny's mom prepared leftover meatloaf from Sunday dinner. Johnny's mom only cooked on the weekends. The rest of the week was filled with leftovers. Johnny finished eating and went upstairs to complete his homework. School was one of the few things he excelled at and was the one thing he could hold over Brock's head. In fact, Johnny knew it was the main reason Brock targeted him. Johnny completed his homework, took a shower, and said his prayers before going to sleep. However, this night Johnny said a special prayer unlike the others. He remembered the story of Samson in the Bible, so he innocently asked God to make him strong like Samson so no one would ever bully him again. He then went to sleep.

The next morning Johnny felt unusually refreshed. He washed up and dressed. He then ate a bowl of his favorite cereal and took a pair of blueberry Pop-Tarts for the road. Johnny kissed his mother goodbye and began the fifteen-minute walk to school. About five minutes in his walk, Johnny noticed his next-door neighbor, Sarah, walking parallel to him across the street. Ever since Johnny could remember, he had a huge crush on Sarah. But Sarah didn't seem to notice. Of course, they were friends, but Johnny could never build up the courage to tell Sarah how he felt. This day was no different.

"Hey, Sarah," he called. "Did you finish the homework Mr. Collins assigned yesterday?"

"Oh hey, Johnny. Yes, I finished it," she replied and proceeded to run and meet up with her friends walking down the street.

"Oh shoot!" Johnny thought. In his rush to leave for school, he had forgotten his calculator. Normally, he would have given it no mind. However, Ms. Kathy from his second-period math class had hinted at a pop quiz today. Johnny was barely holding on to an A in this class and could not afford to bomb on a pop quiz. So he proceeded to run back home to get the calculator. Three minutes later, he was running back to school with calculator in hand. He figured, if he took a shortcut down Espana Court, he would make up enough time to arrive at school without being late. Running full speed, Johnny took a sharp left on Espana Court, and what he saw caused the blood to drain from his face. He made a sudden stop, only twenty feet away from where a mountain lion stood. Announcements were routinely broadcast on the news and at school to be wary of mountain lions roaming neighborhoods. It was not unusual to spot one of these big cats roaming the suburbs, even here in Denver. Johnny knew he was in a pickle. Only a year before, his friend Danny from the adjacent Stony Brooks neighborhood was mauled by a mountain lion. Fortunately for Danny, a state trooper was driving by and was able to scare the mountain lion off with a few warning shots. However, the animal was still able to inflict considerable damage. Danny was in stable condition at the hospital, but it was touch and go when he first arrived in the emergency room. His doctor even told his parents that the staff thought he might not make it that first night. Johnny stood there frozen in fear. He remembered being told to never run when facing a predator like a mountain lion or bear. The beast began to take slow steps toward him. Johnny's mind raced. What was he going to do? The adrenaline mixed with the fear seemed to cloud his mind and judgment. Suddenly, the beast pounced. What happened next would forever change Johnny's destiny. All of a sudden, a surge of power came over him, a power sweet in its essence yet terrifying. It emanated from within him and exploded outward. In that moment, Johnny knew there was no power that could withstand the power now flowing from him. And this realization swept away all fear. He looked at the beast now charging him with a fearlessness that matched the authority he knew he now had over it. In a single motion, Johnny grabbed the lurching animal by the neck and threw it to the ground as if it were rag doll. Now the roles were reversed, and the fear

3

now emanated from the beast. Johnny made a mock roaring noise at the animal, which was enough to cause it to scurry off in the woods.

As suddenly as the power had come upon him, it was gone. Johnny was beside himself.

"What just happened? Did that really just happen?"

He sat there on the curb to gather himself, and as the adrenaline began to subside, he remembered his prayer from the night before.

"Did God really answer my prayer? Do I now have the strength of Samson?" He reasoned, "No, there must be another explanation."

He had watched documentaries of ordinary people exhibiting extraordinary abilities in life or death situations. Johnny concluded that this must have been one of those instances and proceeded to walk to school in a daze. He wondered if he should tell anyone what happened. "No," he thought. They would never believe him.

# II.

Danny sat by himself under his favorite tree, preparing for Mrs. Kathy's promised pop quiz. Danny prided himself on being one of the smartest students at Kingsbury High. In fact, he could think of no one with better grades—that is, except for Johnny. He and Johnny had always been friends. Johnny was one of the few people to visit him in the hospital after his encounter with the mountain lion. Johnny often teased him because of the scar on his arm left by the mountain lion. But Danny knew it was never meant to be mean-spirited. He and Johnny had grown close over the years and often spent late nights studying together—that is, however, until this year, when it appeared Johnny's interest was drawn more toward the opposite sex, particularly Sarah who lived across the street from him. At first, Danny thought nothing of it. But lately, the loneliness that came with not having that

friend around to express shared goals and desires with began to weigh on him. It began as a dark cloud in the distance, but lately, it was threatening to grow into a storm, rushing to overwhelm him. In an unconscious effort at self-preservation, Danny withdrew into himself. The bell for first period rang, and Danny proceeded to make his way to class. He spotted Johnny making his way up the steps and jogged over to join him.

"Hey, Johnny. No time, no see. Where have you been lately?" No response. "Hey, do you want to come over tonight and play video games? I've got some new ones we haven't played together yet. Whadaya say?" Danny thought he saw a nod from Johnny. "Okay, great. I'll see you after school then."

Uplifted by Johnny's nod, Danny made his way to class with the beginnings of a smile. He couldn't remember the last time he smiled.

"Was that Danny I just spoke to? And what was it he just asked me? It sounded like he asked me to come to his house. And I think I nodded yes. What was I thinking? I can't go to his house today. Mom already promised Aunt

Sally that we would come by for dinner," Johnny recalled.

Johnny's Aunt Sally was kind of on the wild side. She colored her hair in purple, pink, and bluish hues and always seemed to be chewing gum. Johnny's mom had two elder brothers and another sister who was younger than them. But she was closest to Aunt Sally who was a year older. Maybe it was because they were only a year apart in age. Johnny was able to get out of going the last time Aunt Sally cooked for them, so he didn't think he'd be able to get out of it this time.

"I'll just tell Danny I can't come by when I see him later today at school," Johnny thought.

# III.

Johnny sat at the dinner table, eating Aunt Sally's famous lasagna. At least that's what Aunt Sally always called it.

"Do you like it, Johnny?" asked Aunt Sally. "You couldn't make it last time, so I made an extra portion for you. How is your friend doing? What's his name again? David? No, Danny."

"Oh shoot!" thought Johnny. He knew there was something he forgot. With his mind still fixated on what happened to him that morning, Johnny had failed to let Danny know he couldn't make it. He would have to make it up to him somehow.

"He's doing okay. I actually turned down a night of video games with him, so I could have some of your famous lasagna."

"I'm glad you two are still friends. Nowadays, good friends are hard to come by," said Aunt Sally.

# IV.

Danny sat on the porch, waiting for Johnny. When the streetlights began to come on, he realized Johnny was going to be a no-show, and he could feel that dark cloud begin to overtake him again. He went inside and turned on the TV. A horror movie marathon was on the tube tonight. Danny didn't like horror movies, and any other time would have changed the channel. However, in his darkened mood, Danny sat passively on the couch and watched one horror movie after another. The very last movie really affected him. It was the story of a young boy who began to dabble in the occult because he believed it would give him power over his enemies. The boy delved deeper and deeper into the occult and began to learn spells that he was able to use to control others.

"I wish I had that kind of power," Danny thought.

Danny turned off the TV and went up to his room for the night. While in his room, Danny went on the Internet and began to research everything he could on spells and magic. His family was not religious and, except for special occasions and holidays, never set foot in a church. So he never gave much consideration to the supernatural. And the occult and any power associated with it was no more real to him than the God Johnny often would talk about. But something about the movie he had watched this night was drawing him to learn more about spells and sorcery. He came across a site that supposedly taught the viewer how to use mind control over others. Danny read and read and became increasingly uneasy as he did. But something seemed to be urging him to continue. Danny recited the last line on the screen out loud as instructed. Suddenly, there was a

loud clapping sound, and the bulb on his lamp blew out. Startled by what happened, Danny immediately turned off the computer and went to bed.

The next morning, he woke up and was reminded of the weird occurrence the night before by the shards of glass that lay on the desk by his computer.

"That was freaky," Danny thought.

As he prepared for school, he shrugged it off and soon forgot all about it. Danny arrived at school and made his way to his first-period class. Out of the corner of his eye, he spotted Johnny, jogging toward him.

"Hey, Danny. Wait up," Johnny called.

Slightly out of breath, Johnny proceeded to apologize for forgetting to come by his house and promised to make it up to him.

"Whatever. Maybe some other time," Danny said.

Johnny agreed they would reschedule some time the following week and continued on to his class. Danny could never stay angry at Johnny for long. He remembered the time they had gotten into a heated argument over a class project. It got so heated that he stormed out of Johnny's house and swore he would never talk to him again. A few days later, they were together again playing catch. Johnny was the only real friend he had, and he did not want to jeopardize it. Danny began to make his way to class but soon found himself stumbling over someone's foot and crashing to the ground.

"Watch where you're going, freak!" Brock laughed as he pulled his foot back and walked away.

Enraged, Danny slowly picked himself off the ground. He was taken aback by the level of anger mixed with hate that was welling up inside of him. He had been angry at Brock before, but it never rose to the level it did now. As Brock made his way down the stairs, Danny thought to himself, "I wish you would stumble over your 'own' feet and fall down those stairs."

Almost as soon as he thought it, he noticed Brock begin to lose his balance and inexplicably started tumbling down the stairs. He no longer saw Brock, but he could hear him moaning as he landed with a thud on his back at the bottom of the stairs.

"Serves you right," thought Danny as he made his way to class.

Danny took his normal seat by the window, and before he could get comfortable, his first-period teacher, Mr. Wiseman, announced that the class would be given a pop quiz.

"Not again! What is it with teachers and pop quizzes?" Danny thought. He was ill-prepared for another quiz and wanted badly to get out of it.

He noticed the mug of coffee Mr. Wiseman always brought to class sitting next to the stack of test handouts. He then thought to himself, "I wish Mr. Wiseman would knock his coffee over onto those tests."

Without warning, Mr. Wiseman made an awkward turn to his desk and knocked the coffee directly onto the tests.

"Oh shucks! Looks like there won't be a pop quiz today after all," said Mr. Wiseman.

"That's great!" thought Danny.

The rest of the school day was relatively uneventful. The bell for the end of final period finally rang, and Danny gladly began the twenty-minute walk back home. He decided to stop by the convenience store that was on the way to buy a pack of gum.

"Let me see if I remember where the gum is at this store. If I recall, it should be the second aisle toward the back."

Danny proceeded toward the back of the store, but he heard a commotion near the front by the cash register. Danny peeked over the aisle, and to his horror, he noticed the store being robbed. He quickly ducked down, hoping he wasn't noticed. But he was too slow.

"Hey, you behind the aisle. Come over here," the robber called out.

Danny slowly made his way to the front of the store with his hands above his head. He noticed the thief was about his height, and though his face was covered by a Hulk mask, his other features and mannerisms suggested he couldn't be much older than himself. Something about this person's voice was strangely familiar to Danny. The tattoo of skull

and bones on his left arm confirmed Danny's suspicion. This was Kevin who had graduated the year before. Kevin was the other tormentor that made Danny's time at school unbearable. He remembered the time Kevin and Brock teamed up against him and tried to stuff his head into the bathroom toilet. And they would have succeeded if Johnny had not walked in to distract them. Johnny threatened to run and get Principal Jim if they didn't let Danny go, and after some minor roughhousing, Kevin and Brock complied.

"Give me all the money in the cash register!" Kevin shouted.

Danny stood with his hands above his head and watched with an anger and hate that seemed to rise from inside of him. But the anger and hate had nothing to do with the fact that Kevin was robbing the place. Instead, the anger and hate came as he remembered all the times Kevin tormented him over the last three years. Kevin was using a bowgun to rob the store, and Danny thought to himself, "Only an idiot would use a bowgun to rob someone."

As Kevin waved the bowgun in the cashier's face, Danny thought to himself, "I wish this jerk would shoot himself in the foot."

Suddenly, something compelled Kevin to look Danny's way and, with a glazed look, proceed to point the bow toward his foot and pull the trigger.

Kevin immediately dropped the bowgun and screamed, "My foot! My foot! I shot my foot!" while hopping around the store on one foot with the arrow sticking out the other. Danny couldn't help but laugh at the sight. He'd watched numerous comedies where the bumbling thief wounded himself in a similar manner, but he never thought he would see it happen in real life. The cashier, a large burly man in his fifties, called the cops and secured Kevin while attending to his wound. The cops soon arrived, followed by the ambulance. After a few questions from the police, Danny made his way out of the store and continued his walk home.

As he walked by the ambulance, he heard Kevin scream toward him, "You did this to me, Danny! You did this! I don't know how! But I know you did it!"

"What was Kevin talking about? I did this to him?" Danny thought.

Suddenly, he remembered the weird events from the night before. He then recalled Brock falling down the stairs and Mr. Wiseman knocking his coffee over.

"All these events happened after I wished them."

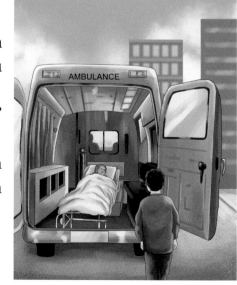

He also remembered something else. In every instance, each of these individuals seemed to look straight at him with a glazed look in their eyes just before the "accidents."

"Surely, I had nothing to do with this. These were all freak accidents," Danny thought.

He decided to formulate a test to determine if he, indeed, had the ability to control the minds of others. The next day he went back to the store and noticed two students from his school who were into that "Goth thing." Recently, it seemed like more and more students were being drawn into the Goth subculture. Both of these teens were dressed all in pitch-black. He walked slowly down the aisle across the teens and noticed one was smoking a cigarette. He then purposely thought to himself, "Burn your friend in the arm with the cigarette butt."

The teen with the cigarette turned toward Danny with that same glazed look and, without hesitation, burned his friend's arm with the cigarette butt.

"Dude! What's your problem?" the other teen yelled.

"I'm sorry, man. I don't know what came over me," the teen with the cigarette said.

Danny was beside himself. "Could this be true? Do I now have the power of mind control," he thought.

Danny made his way home and, like a kid in the movie, began to delve deeper and deeper into spells and enchantments online. At first, it was all fun and games. Danny would count down the hours when the school day would end so he could spend more time on his computer. But what began as a game soon became an obsession. Danny could feel himself losing control. It was as though another was taking over his will. He found himself snapping at others for the smallest infraction. He also found himself being drawn to dark places and avoiding brightly lit rooms. In fact, now he never went anywhere without wearing dark sunglasses that completely hid his eyes. "What's going on with me?" Danny thought.

In the back of his mind, he knew it had something to do with all the time he was now spending online researching and learning new spells. But he simply couldn't stop. He'd heard stories of those suffering from addiction to things like drugs and gambling. But he never took such stories seriously—until now. The lust for power had become Danny's drug. And he was growing addicted to it. The ecstasy that came over him when someone obeyed his suggestions only pulled him deeper and deeper into the darkness. However, Danny noticed something peculiar about his abilities. He did not seem to have the ability to control the minds of those he and other students liked to call Bible thumpers. One day Danny decided he was going to use his new powers on Johnny. He noticed that Johnny regularly stopped by Sarah's locker after the final period. Danny's plan was to wait for Johnny to walk over to Sarah and then use his power to cause Johnny to insult her.

"Maybe if Sarah became angry with Johnny, he and I could spend more time together like we used to," Danny thought.

Johnny walked over to Sarah's locker as expected, and Danny thought, "Tell her that her breath stinks." But instead of the glazed look and the immediate response to obey that he received from others, Johnny's eyes seemed to pierce right through him as though he knew what Danny was thinking. Danny turned away.

# V.

Johnny was beginning to spend more and more time with Sarah. The week before they were assigned as partners, tasked at working together on the annual student science project. Today they had agreed to meet in the science room. Sarah always knew Johnny had a crush on her, but she never looked at him in this way—that is, until this year. There seemed to be something different about Johnny. She did not quite know what it was, but she was becoming attracted to it.

"How much you want to bet I can throw this ball of paper in that trash bin?" Johnny asked.

"I'll let you take me to the movies if you make it," she replied.

Flushed and flustered by the unexpected response, Johnny missed the trash bin by nearly ten feet. Both began to laugh about it until Sarah noticed the ball of paper had knocked over a glass of flammable liquid onto a lit Bunsen burner. Before either could react, the entire counter was in flames. Johnny immediately ran for the fire extinguisher, but he soon realized that all the chemicals in the room was causing the fire to spread faster than it could be contained. He then grabbed Sarah's hand, and both ran to the door. But to their horror, someone had locked the door from the outside. The high school was one of the few in the state where the classrooms could only be locked and unlocked from the outside. Apparently, Sarah and Johnny had spent more time in the classroom than they realized, and someone had locked the door, not realizing they were there. Both began to knock furiously at the door and scream for help. Unfortunately for them, most of the students had already left for the day, and the remaining teachers and staff were congregating in the teachers' lounge, which was on the other side of the school property. Johnny considered breaking a window. Unfortunately, this was one of the few classrooms with no windows. Johnny could feel the heat begin to rise as the grim realization that there was no way out hit him. Johnny looked over to Sarah who was still holding his hand, and he knew, by the fear in her eyes, that she had come to the same realization. He then noticed something that caused the blood to drain from his face. The flames had engulfed the gas tank in the corner of the room. He knew that within moments the tank could explode. Suddenly, the same surge of power that he felt when he faced the mountain lion came over him again. He then instructed Sarah to stand close to him. Sarah looked over to Johnny and noticed a fire in his eyes that seemed to burn brighter than the fire surrounding them. She then witnessed something that should not have been possible. In a single motion, Johnny took hold of metal handles welded into the metal doors and

proceeded to rip the doors from their hinges. He then turned instinctively toward the blaze while holding the doors in a vice grip between them and the fire. Almost immediately after doing so, the tank exploded. The shock wave was so great that everything in the classroom was obliterated. Even the doors to the classroom across the hall were blown off their hinges, and the windows within that classroom had shattered. Sarah watched in amazement as time seemed to slow down and go in slow motion. Everything around her was being shaken and ripped apart, but Johnny stood immovable by her side with two enormous doors in his arms as the blast of flames rushed on either side of them.

# VI.

It didn't take long for news of the blast to travel around school. The six-o-clock evening news showed images of the devastation created by the blast in several of the rooms along the hallway. Both Sarah and Johnny were interviewed by the beat reporter for the nightly news. Johnny thought how strange it was to watch himself on television.

"This is Jane reporting for the six-o-clock evening news. I have here with me Johnny and Sarah who recently went through a harrowing event in the school's science lab and are lucky to be alive to talk about it. Some of the school staff who were the first to arrive on the scene after hearing the blast state that they found both of you frozen in place while Johnny held two huge metal doors in both arms. Can you explain to the people how you survived such a large blast while everything around you was obliterated?"

Johnny recounted the events that led up to the blast, how he was able to remove the doors from their hinges and the blast that soon followed.

"But, Johnny," replied the reporter, "those doors are made of solid metal that are held in place by metal hinges. Is it humanly impossible for anyone to do what you described, especially for someone of your size? You cannot be more the five-foot-six and 140 pounds."

Sarah then interrupted the reporter and explained how everything that Johnny said was true because she was there beside him when it occurred. Johnny fumbled for words in an attempt to further describe what happened. When he began to attribute his sudden strength to a prayer he made to God weeks earlier to make him strong like Samson in the Bible, he was abruptly cut off by the reporter.

"Well, there you have it, folks. The story of the man-boy who used his bare hands to rip off doors of iron to save himself and his friend. Or shall we call him Little Samson?"

The next day Johnny noticed the stares and could hear faint whispers of "Little Samson" from the other students as he walked the hallways.

# VII.

Following the incident, it seemed as though Sarah and Johnny were inseparable. They studied together, ate lunch together, and even walked to school together. Their growing relationship had not gone unnoticed by others, least of all by Brock. Brock had always considered Sarah one of "his girls," and he was growing increasingly jealous of the time Sarah and Johnny were spending together. Years before, Johnny had confided in Sarah about how his mother often had to buy their clothing from the local Salvation Army. Sarah later shared this information with Brock when she was actually one of "his girls." That time had long since passed, but Brock decided he would now use this information against Johnny.

One day, after school, he and his friends stayed behind, and when no one else was around, they spray-painted the words "SALVATION JOHNNY" in red and white paint all over Johnny's locker. They then placed several pictures on his locker of Johnny and his mom coming out of the local Salvation Army. The next morning, when Johnny arrived at school, he noticed the strange looks and snickering from other students in the hallway. His faced turned red with embarrassment when he came to his locker. He knew immediately who was responsible. But how did Brock know about his secret? He confided in only two people about his secret. He once told Danny, but it wasn't in Danny's nature to bully others in this way. The only other person he told was Sarah, and the realization that Sarah was responsible for sharing this information to Brock hit him like a ton of bricks. He looked over to Sarah who was standing by her locker as she shamefully looked away.

He then looked toward Brock who had a mocking grin on his face. The only thing Johnny could think of for the rest of the day was how he was going to get back at Brock and his friends. He then decided what he was going to do. That night he took numerous Carolina Reaper peppers and squeezed the juice into a jar. The next day, while Brock and his crew were at football practice, Johnny sneaked into the football locker room and smeared the juice all over their large bath towels.

Johnny scarcely had time to leave the locker room before Brock and his crew returned.

"Did you see the look on Johnny's face when he saw his locker?" said Kent. Kent was one of Brock's closest friends. The two did everything together and were seldom seen apart from each other.

"Yeah. He looked like he was going to cry," replied Brock.

"Hey, Brock. Do you smell something funny?" asked Kent.

"Not really. The cafeteria is next door. Maybe it's something they're preparing," responded Brock.

Both boys and the rest of the crew proceeded to take showers, thinking nothing else of it. Johnny waited patiently outside the locker room to see what would happen. He listened as the showers turned off one by one, and Brock, along with the others, proceeded to dry themselves off with the Reaper-smeared towels. The first one to voice concern was Kent.

"Hey, Brock. Is it hot in here, or is it just me?"

"No, bro. It is unusually hot in here. Oh my goodness! I'm burning up!" replied Brock.

Johnny chuckled as he heard Brock and his crew run back into the showers like foxes with their tails on fire to try and cool off. He could hear them all screaming, "It's so hot! Make it stop!"

After several minutes, the screaming slowly died down as each one was able to wash the pepper juice off their bodies. Johnny thought he had gotten away with it until they all came out of the locker room. From head to toe, Brock and his crew were as red as fully ripe tomatoes. When Johnny

19

saw them, he busted out laughing. Unfortunately for Johnny, Brock saw him laughing and put two and two together.

"GET HIM!" shouted Brock.

Johnny took off running toward the football field with Brock and his crew in hot pursuit. Johnny made it to the practice field with Brock and his crew closing fast. He then realized he had no chance at outrunning his pursuers, so he turned to face them. Taken aback by this sudden display of boldness, Brock and his crew also stopped.

"Five against one hardly seems like a fair fight," said Johnny.

"Okay. Here's what we're going to do," replied Brock. "We have a drill in football we like to call the gauntlet. If you can make it past the five of us in the gauntlet, we'll let you go. You see those cones in the middle of the field? That's where the gauntlet will take place. If you run outside of those cones, we have official permission to pummel you."

*How am I going to get out of this mess?* Johnny thought. *I'm going to get pummeled either way, so I might as well take my chances and run for it.*

Right before he was going to take off, he heard a voice on the inside tell him, "Do not run." The voice then said, 'Play with them but do no harm. Do good. Do no harm."

*Do good? Do no harm? Where did that come from? Now I'm hearing voices,* Johnny thought.

Johnny brushed it off as his heightened imagination but took it as a sign.

"Okay, Brock. I'll play your game. Lead the way."

Johnny encouraged himself by remembering the incident with the mountain lion and the incident with the metal doors. It then occurred to him that these five brutes didn't stand a chance. Johnny walked toward the gauntlet or, more precisely, was pushed from behind toward it. When they arrived, Brock and his crew, each outweighing Johnny by over 100 pounds, lined up 10 yards apart from one another. Johnny watched patiently as they made it to their spots. He then picked up the football and asked confidently, "You guys ready?"

When he took the first step toward his first challenger, he didn't feel the power that came over him as the other times. This time he felt an overwhelming sense of joy. As though he could leap a mountain or run one hundred miles an hour. He began to jog slowly and gradually increased his speed. The first boy in the gauntlet looked on with

excitement in his eyes, the kind of excitement a wolf might have right before chumping down on a slab of raw meat. When Johnny was within a yard of the boy, he made a move so fast that it left the boy tangled in a twisted heap as though he were playing twister with himself. The second boy watched with alarm and with slightly less confidence than he had a few seconds earlier. Johnny spotted the doubt in his eyes and fed off it. He sped up, but this time, instead of maneuvering around him, he ran right by him. The second challenger recognized the tactic at the last second and grabbed a hold of Johnny's shirt. But reminiscent to the famous scene of Earl Campbell dragging defenders while his jersey was

being ripped off, Johnny dragged the second boy nearly 5 yards until the T-shirt he was wearing ripped off. He did the same to the third boy. The fourth boy expected the same, but at the last second, Johnny hurdled him with the grace only found in Olympic

sprinters. He then came face-to-face with Brock who was the last challenger in the gauntlet. Johnny slowed down and found himself remembering all the times Brock had humiliated him. He decided then and there that he was going to return the favor. As the anger within him rose, it replaced the joy that was once there. Seething, Johnny planned on doing to Brock what he did to the mountain lion. Brock watched the anger in Johnny's face and could actually sense a bit of fear on the inside. Both boys began to run toward each other, and the two collided with a thud. Shocked and bewildered, Brock found himself on his back with the air knocked out of him.

Johnny then heard the same inner voice say, "Do you feel any better for teaching Brock a lesson?"

"No. I actually don't," replied Johnny in his mind.

He then heard the voice say, "You will soon learn that your greatest fulfillment will only come from obeying my instructions."

Brock stood up in a rage and in a fighting stance. But before he could take a swing at Johnny, Coach Miller could be heard from the sideline, yelling, "Enough!"

Apparently, Coach Miller was watching everything that transpired. Coach Miller was the multitalented coach who did a little bit of everything for the school. When he wasn't coaching, he was preparing the lesson for his second-period history class. Johnny stood to his feet as Coach Miller walked over to the group. "What's all this, Brock?"

Brock proceeded to make up a story, but Coach Miller stopped him mid-sentence. "Stop while you're ahead. I know about what you guys did to Johnny's locker. You're going to clean up his locker before you leave today. By the way, the five of you will be volunteering at the local Salvation Army for the next eight weekends. Maybe then you'll gain some appreciation for the work these people do."

He then pulled Johnny to the side. "Johnny boy. Or should I call you Little Samson? You looked good out there. Have you ever played any organized sports?"

Johnny was about to say, "Yeah. In my dreams." But he thought better of it and said, "Only flag football on our intramural league."

"Well," said Coach Miller, "how would you like to play on the varsity football team? I can't guarantee you'll be given any playing time. We already have two seniors who alternate at running back, which is the position I want to try you out at."

Johnny thought about it. *Me, on the varsity football team, how cool would that be? And my friends would never believe it!*

It only took Johnny a few seconds to accept the invitation.

The next few days at school, however, were intolerable for Johnny. What had always been playful banter between he and Brock had turned into real hatred. In fact, the two had to be separated on multiple occasions to prevent full-out brawls. And the satisfaction Johnny always thought he would feel by humiliating Brock never came. In fact, he wished he could go back to that moment in the gauntlet and change what he did. He now realized his actions did not bring him the vindication he desired because he had behaved no different from Brock. He had, in fact, become Brock, and he hated that he had allowed his emotions to get the better of him. He would later try on multiple occasions to apologize, but Brock would have nothing of it.

The next week Johnny met Coach Miller in the weight room, and Coach Miller showed him around. To their credit, the players in the weight room were nothing like the jerk, ego maniacs Johnny always envisioned them.

"Hey, Johnny. I heard you were going to be joining us," said Blake. Blake was the star wide receiver on the team and was already being looked at by several division I colleges around the country. "By the way, I heard what you did to Brock and the rest of them. Way to go." Johnny received a similar welcome from the other players he met.

Coach Miller then showed where his football locker would be and ordered the trainer to provide him with the required pads and practice uniform. Johnny participated in his first practice the following day. The team was separated by position. Those who participated on the offense were on one half of the field, while those whose position was on defense were on the other half of the field. Johnny was happy about this because it meant he could avoid Brock. But he knew this would only be temporary. Eventually, the offense and defense would come together to scrimmage against each other. Johnny joined the running backs as expected and participated in all the drills. It was one of the most grueling experiences he could remember, and the fact that he was out of shape did not help. In fact, Coach Miller warned him to anticipate as much, but he encouraged him not to become discouraged by it and that it would become easier as his conditioning gradually improved. It turned out the coach was correct. It also turned out that Johnny was a natural at the sport. He was always a standout on the intramural leagues, but he never thought it would actually translate on the varsity football team. His natural quickness served him well against the other players on the intramural leagues, but he was finding himself having the same success against college-recruited players on the varsity team that he never thought possible.

Coach Miller took notice and realized Johnny's exploits against Brock and the other boys was no fluke. He then made Johnny the lead returner on the kickoff return team for the upcoming game on Friday. It seems Brock and his friends also took notice, and the taunts and verbal abuse they constantly directed his way during those first few weeks of scrimmages gradually died down. In fact, Brock actually defended Johnny when one of

the members of his crew began to taunt him after a play during a recent scrimmage.

Johnny could not sleep the night before Friday's game. He found himself staring at the ceiling, going over the different kick return plays the team practiced during the week. Return right, return left, middle return, reverse, fake reverse, lateral, double lateral, etc. were all plays the return team practiced over and over. Johnny could remember watching these returns from the stands, but he never imagined how much planning and practicing went into mastering them. From the blocking schemes to how and where the kick returner needed to run, there was a science to the apparent madness, which fascinated him.

Game night finally arrived. When the team returned to the locker room after pregame warm-ups, Coach Miller recited a popular poem by the late coach of the Green Bay Packers, Vince Lombardi. The coach then said a prayer for both teams. After the prayer, there was still about fifteen minutes before the teams would storm the field to their respective sidelines.

Johnny found the wait intolerable. He could think of no other time when he was so nervous. About five minutes in the wait, he found himself throwing up over the locker room toilet. As he walked out of the bathroom a little embarrassed, Brock walked up to him and patted him on the back. He then told him, "Don't be embarrassed. It means you're ready to play."

Johnny walked out of the locker room into the cool brisk autumn air. Johnny always enjoyed autumn. In the past, he had heard others say it's starting to feel like football weather. This now took on a new personal meaning for him. The team gathered by the goal post with Coach Miller at the lead. They then ran as a unit with a shout to their sideline. Johnny took it all in. He was fascinated by the shape and position of the night lights. With deeper interest, he watched the actions of the players and coaches of the opposing team. He observed the fans in the stands, looking to see if he could see his mom or any of his friends. He didn't find his mom among the crowd, but he did see Sarah who was smiling at him with a thumbs-up. Johnny smiled back, and the interaction seemed to calm his nerves. The captains of the two teams met midfield for the coin toss, and Kingsbury won the toss, choosing to receive the kick. The special teams coach then gathered the players on the kick return team and informed them to run "return right" while looking at Johnny. Johnny and the rest of the players nodded and proceeded to run out onto the field. Johnny watched with nervous energy as the opposing team lined up to kickoff. Before he knew it, the ball was in the air, coming toward him. As he went over the blocking scheme for "return right" in his mind, the same joy came over him that he experienced during the gauntlet with Brock and his crew. Johnny caught the ball, and everything slowed down before him. It was as though he could see what would happen before it did. While everyone else saw the chaos of players from the two teams clashing together, Johnny clearly saw the path that would lead to the endzone. He could not explain it, but he instinctively ran toward it. However, the path Johnny envisioned did not match the plan

drawn up by the coaches. As Johnny began to run, he could hear the coaches screaming, "You're running the wrong way!" Johnny ignored the voices and ran where he believed his feet and legs were being directed.

As Johnny ran, the path that moments before was blocked by opposing players suddenly opened up, and with a burst of speed that surprised both fans and players alike, he left opposing players grabbing at air. His coaches who before were screaming that he was going the wrong way were now screaming for him to keep running. Before he knew it, Johnny was by himself with no one between him and the endzone. Out of the corner of his eye, he could see the fans standing up and urging him on. Johnny watched as the 50-yard line passed by, the 40, the 30, the 20, the 10, and finally, he crossed over the goal line. He turned around out of breath and met his teammates who came to congratulate him. As he ran toward the sideline, he could hear the fans repeating the words, "Samson, Samson, Samson . . ."

# VIII.

Danny watched alone from the stands as the crowd chanted, "Samson, Samson." He always knew Johnny possessed athletic ability. He had witnessed his exploits often during the intramural football games. But he never expected this. Johnny not only showed that he could play on the varsity team, but he also showed that he just might be one of the better players. Danny watched in silence and began to feel what he could only describe as rejection from and bitterness toward Johnny. Johnny had always been the one person he could confide in and express his dismay toward the way others treated him, especially the jocks on the football team. But now it seemed he was losing that one person from his life. And worst of all, that person was becoming the very object of his persecution.

The following Monday morning Danny was met by Johnny in front of school before their first-period class. Danny noticed the excitement in Johnny's eyes as he proceeded to gush about Friday's game.

"Did you see the game?" asked Johnny.

"Yeah, I saw it," replied Danny in an even tone.

"Well, what did you think?" replied Johnny who proceeded to spend the next five minutes excitedly explaining every single detail from that night.

Danny listened in silence and, when it appeared Johnny was finished, simply said, "I have to go, I'm late for class," and walked away.

Johnny watched in silence as Danny walked away, not sure what to make of what just happened.

After school, Danny began to spend time researching different wizardry sites online as he normally did, but ten minutes into his search, he slumped over his desk and slammed his fist against the desk. How could Johnny do this to him? Of all people, he never expected Johnny to turn on him. Now it seemed the whole world was against him. He then decided to visit a social site on the Internet for those who were into wizardry and spells. He had come across the site before but never spent time scrolling through it. However, this night he searched it out and began to read over many of the blogs. Most of the blogs he read had to do with Harry Potter, its characters, and what new story line could be expected in the next installment. But one of the blogs caught his interest. As he read, the message appeared to mirror what he had experienced since the night he had spoken the spell in his room that seemed to give him his powers. He responded to the blog with his own message, and soon he and his new "friend" began to strike up a long conversation. Hours passed by, but it seemed like only minutes because he had become so engaged in the conversation. Danny realized what time it was and decided to sign off so he would not be exhausted in the morning.

After school, he immediately completed his homework so that he would have more time to spend blogging with his new online friend. Feeling comfortable revealing aspects of his life, Danny proceeded to reveal the details of how he was able to control the actions of others simply by thinking about it. His friend responded by saying he too exercised this power and had taken it a step farther. He then explained how he had come across a site that taught the viewer how to control animals. Intrigued by this, Danny proceeded to obtain the address for the website so he too could learn about this new power. Danny visited the site, absorbing everything that he read. At the end of the site were spells the reader was encouraged to repeat to obtain this new power. Remembering his experience the first time he read a spell out loud, Danny was hesitant to do it over again. However, the lure of more power drove Danny to obey, and he proceeded to repeat the spell. Danny waited for something to happen, like a loud sound or exploding light bulbs. However,

nothing happened. Danny concluded the spell didn't work and decided to call it a night.

The next morning Danny new something had happened to him. He didn't know what, but he was not the same boy who had gone to bed. He had changed. He looked in the mirror, and everything appeared the same, except his eyes. Danny had always had greenish-blue eyes. But as he looked in the mirror, the color of his eyes had changed to black and not the black you typically associate with black. This black was pitch-black that seemed to pierce his soul. Not only had the color of his eyes changed, but the empathy that once resided in his heart had vanished also.

A coldness had settled in him, and he knew he was now capable of a cruelty that at one time he would have fought against. The first person who came to mind was Brock. It was time for Brock to pay, and Danny was going to use this new power to make him. Danny glanced down at the scars on his arm and knew exactly what animal he would use to exact his revenge. He was going to use a mountain lion, which had caused him so much pain, to inflict the same pain on his enemy.

The following weekend Danny made up a lie to his parents about spending the weekend in the mountains with Johnny. Danny then loaded his backpack with enough food and camping supplies to spend the night in the mountains and made the two-hour bike ride up into the mountains. There were certain areas that campers were warned to avoid because of the many sightings of mountain lions and bears over the years, but Danny proceeded to set up camp exactly in the area campers were encouraged to avoid.

Danny brought a slab of raw beef from home that he intended to use to lure the animal to him. He placed the raw beef next to a tree approximately 20 yards away from his camp and sat down to wait.

As midnight approached, Danny began to feel his eyes become heavy as sleep overtook him. It seemed he had only slept a few minutes when he heard a rustling in the grass. He opened his eyes to see a huge brown bear sniffing the meat. It then occurred to him that in his eagerness to come up to the mountain to use his new power, he never tested himself to see if he, indeed, had this new power.

The bear noticed Danny's movement and spotted him out of the corner of its eyes. Danny recognized that he was spotted and caught something else out of the corner of his own eyes. To his horror, the bear was female, and she had two cubs behind her. Danny heard stories of people being mauled to death by female bears protecting their young, and before he knew it, the bear was charging him. Danny stood up and realized at that moment that the loss of empathy not only extended to others but to himself as well. He could care less if he lived or died and simply faced the charging beast and said, "Stop."

The bear immediately stopped and stood there bewildered, not understanding why it stopped. It looked at Danny, and everything in him wanted to charge what appeared to be an easy meal, but its feet seemed stuck to the ground.

Emboldened by this, Danny walked over to the animal and then told it to back up. The animal immediately obeyed. He noticed they were close to the side of a mountain and, with no care for the animal or the cubs with it, told the bear to run toward the mountain. The animal then turned and ran full speed toward the side of the mountain and slammed head first against it, knocking itself out cold.

Danny watched in amazement as his newfound power did its work. He then approached the slab of beef to make sure it was not eaten by the bear and scared the cubs away.

After he was sure the meat was still intact, he went back to his camp site and waited for his intended prey. It did not take long because within an hour, he noticed a large mountain lion slowly approach the slab of meat. Danny stood up, not caring if he was heard by the mountain lion. The mountain lion noticed him and was startled by his actions. Danny casually walked forward, which the mountain lion saw as strange behavior for a creature it normally saw as potential prey. Not sure what to make of this creature before him, the mountain lion attempted to make itself as intimidating and imposing as possible by bearing its large canines and flaring its back. This seemed to only infuriate Danny, which brought back memories of the day he was nearly mauled to death. For a moment, Danny considered giving the mountain lion the same fate he had given the bear, but he thought better of it. He then commanded the mountain lion to run alongside of him as he rode his bike to the junkyard located a mile from his home. He then locked the animal in an old abandoned cage he discovered a few days before. He

then made his way home and waited for his opportunity. He didn't have to wait long.

# IX.

Midterms were scheduled to take place in two days, and everyone dreaded Ms. Kathy's math exam. Ms. Kathy was notorious for giving the most difficult exam in school. And though the scores were graded on a curve, the average score was never higher than a C-. Brock's friend, Kent, decided it would be different this year. Kent devised a scheme to steal the answer key from Ms. Kathy's office.

One day he noticed Ms. Kathy place the key to her office in a secret compartment behind a picture on the classroom wall. Ms. Kathy thought she was alone, but she was not aware that Kent was watching through a crack in the door. Kent then devised a scheme to steal the answer key when she was not there.

That morning Kent attempted to bring Brock into their plans.

"Hey, Brock. We're going to steal the answer key to Ms. Kathy's exam tomorrow during lunch . . . You're coming with us?"

"I believe I'm going to pass," said Brock. He didn't know why, but ever since his amiable association with Johnny started, the childish pranks he often took part in began to end.

"Okay. Do you mind if I keep your hat until tomorrow?" asked Kent who borrowed Brock's hat the day before.

"Sure. No problem," replied Brock.

The next day Kent and two other boys watched for when Ms. Kathy would leave for lunch. After it was confirmed Ms. Kathy had left, the three boys went into the classroom and removed the key from the secret compartment. They then proceeded to break into her office and steal the answer key. The boys intended to make a copy of the answer key and replace it along with the key to the office before Ms. Kathy returned from lunch. However, Ms. Kathy made an unexpected return to the classroom to retrieve documents she intended to share with a colleague during lunch.

One of the boys assigned to watch sounded the alarm. Kent estimated that he only had a few seconds before they were discovered, so instead of replacing the answer key and the office key, he and the other boys rushed out of the classroom with both items in hand.

However, in his hurry to leave the classroom, the hat Kent was wearing that belonged to Brock flew off, landing on the floor in Ms. Kathy's office.

# X.

Ms. Kathy walked into the classroom and noticed the door to her office was open. "Did I leave this door open?" she thought.

She then noticed the hat on the floor and realized her office was broken into. She checked to see if everything was in place and discovered that the answer key to the midterm exam was missing. When she checked to see if the office key was located in its secret compartment, she found that it too was missing. An investigation was immediately initiated, and the main piece of evidence was Brock's hat. It did not take long to surmise who the owner of the hat was, and Brock soon found himself being questioned in Principal Jim's office.

After being drilled with multiple questions by Principal Jim and Ms. Kathy in an attempt to make him confess, Brock was close to informing them who actually stole the answer key. However, in the end, he simply told them that he did not do it. Brock's past reputation did not help his cause, and he was suspended for three days by Principal Jim. Principal Jim expressed how he intended to have him expelled. However, Johnny intervened on Brock's behalf and convinced Principal Jim that Brock was actually changing and deserved leniency.

After leaving Principal Jim's office, Brock met Johnny at his locker and expressed thanks for putting in a good word for him. Brock's father was a former military and one of the few people Brock actually feared. From the time he was a youth, Brock's father spent countless hours helping him develop his skills as a football player. Brock's father fully intended for him to be offered a football scholarship at a major college program by the time he graduated, and Brock was on track to do just that. Schools such as LSU, USC, Washington, and Texas were all showing strong interest, and this would have all been derailed had he been expelled.

While talking to Johnny, Kent walked up to Brock to tell him he was sorry for what happened. But Brock was having none of it. He was furious that Kent had not admitted his guilt after finding out he was suspended. But Kent had a similar relationship with his father, and fear prevented him from doing what he knew was the right thing to do. When Kent refused to come clean to Principal Jim at Brock's urging, Brock became even more infuriated and nearly struck Kent. Instead, he punched the locker next to Kent, leaving a huge dent, and stormed off.

Brock and Kent had been best friends since their childhood, and it hurt Johnny to see the rift this had created between them. Pain and regret could also be seen in Kent's face after Brock stormed off as he slowly walked away to his next class.

# XI.

Danny lay in his bed, looking up at the ceiling. He knew he was changing. He reflected upon the apathy he felt toward himself when he faced the bear and the mountain lion and could feel that same apathy grow for the people around him. He found himself snapping at his mother, which he had never done, on a regular basis. Other than Johnny, Danny's mother was the only person he could truly call friend, and he could feel himself growing distant from her in the same way he and Johnny had grown distant.

Today's argument with his mother was probably the worse. Danny's mother was waiting for him by the door as he arrived home from school.

"Danny, we need to talk," spoke his mother.

"About what, Mom? I'm tired, and I just want to go to my room," snapped Danny.

"About your behavior lately. We've always been able to talk. But recently, I've noticed how you've become withdrawn from everyone, including me. I've noticed you've even stopped hanging around Johnny. You two have always been close. Tell me, what's going on? What can I do to help?" said his mom.

Danny could feel the wall that had developed between them begin to come down. But immediately, the coldness within him went to work rebuilding it.

"My behavior is fine, Mom. If you would take some time with your head outside of your Bible, maybe you would notice," retorted Danny.

"It's because of the time that I spend in my Bible that I know something very dark has come over you. The Lord spoke to me and told me to look at your computer. What I found is very disturbing. I found several sites about casting spells, mind control, witchcraft. These sites are extremely dangerous. How long have you been visiting them?" probed his mother.

At this, Danny became visibly enraged. "What right have you to go through my personal stuff?

And don't speak to me about the Lord. Where was he when Dad died?" shouted Danny. "I don't need God. I have all the power I will ever need."

Danny's mother became visibly shaken after hearing this.

"What do you mean, you have all the power you will ever need? Don't trust the devil's lies, son. He will promise you the world, but in the end, you will only have misery and loss. Please don't continue down this path."

Danny turned away in a rage and stormed up to his room, slamming the door behind him. Danny's mother watched helplessly and went to her room to pray.

Danny replayed the argument over and over in his head as he lay on his bed. As he began to dose off, in between sleeping and waking, he heard something in him say, "Don't listen to her, I'll be your father. I've already marked your eyes. I will now mark your hands. So long as you have this mark, you are mine, and I will give you all the power you will ever need."

Danny blew it off as his imagination and went to sleep.

The next morning he awoke with a burning sensation in the palms of his hands. He dismissed it as lack of blood flow while he slept and prepared himself for school.

# XII.

Danny went through the school day on autopilot. It was as if he was there but not there. He sat in philosophy class looking out the window, thinking about the argument he had with his mother the night before. Did he really hear a voice tell him he would be his father and give him all the power he needed? Or was it his imagination running wild? While contemplating on this, he immediately heard the same voice say, "I am real and will give you all the power you will ever need. I will make these people puppets in your hands if you serve me."

The discussion in history class was on world religions and their influence on society.

"Does God exist? And if He does, how can you prove it? All the major religions believe in some form of deity. How do we know which is right? Or are all they all right?" asked the teacher. The teacher gave them a moment to think about it, fairly sure no one would respond.

Before she continued to speak, Charlotte, whom Danny recognized as one of the known Bible thumpers in school, spoke up. "Well, it is illogical to believe they are all right. That makes no sense. If God exists, He would make a way for the people He created to know who He was, kind of like the signature of God. How do you recognize someone you have not seen? You know them by their voice. There are people who create deep, personal relationships with those they have never seen simply by reading their words and hearing their voice. There are martyrs in the Christian faith, both in the Bible and modern day, who went to their deaths for their faith because they heard the voice of the One in whom they believed."

The other students listened intently, and many began to nod in agreement.

As Danny sat and listened, he heard the same voice say, "Tell the children to rebel."

Danny had never attempted to control the behavior of multiple people at the same time. It had always been single individuals and animals. Could he really do this? He then heard the voice say, "Speak over the students with your thoughts."

Danny obeyed the voice and began to mentally suggest to the students that what Charlotte was saying was bigoted, untrue, and narrow-minded. He could sense the atmosphere in the room grow dark, and one by one, other students began to speak out against what Charlotte was saying.

One of the students even stood up out of her chair and began screaming at Charlotte, saying, "How could you be so narrow-minded? By saying Christianity is the one true faith, you summarily dismiss all the other faiths as being false. What gives you the right to make such a claim? What about the billions of Muslims and Hindus who don't believe as you do? This is why these martyrs you celebrate were killed! They spoke against the beliefs of others by suggesting their faith was a fraud!"

When the teacher realized she was losing the class, she abruptly ended the discussion and went on to another subject.

But like someone experiencing a high from a drug, Danny was intoxicated by this new power. He was now able to control large groups of people, and the feeling made him want more.

# XIII.

Charlotte sat in class dumbfounded by how the students suddenly turned on her. Not all the students attacked her. The students she recognized as regulars at the weekly FCA meetings remained silent. And there were a handful she did not recognize who remained neutral. However, majority of the students turned on her. It was as if someone had flipped a switch. She did notice a student in the corner of the room staring intensely at her. Something about the darkness in his eyes unsettled her. It was a sinister look as though he was taking pleasure in what was taking place. She would have to watch out for him. Something told her there was more going on with him than meets the eyes. And it wasn't good.

Still trying to regain her composure after what had suddenly happened, she remembered a teaching one of the guest speakers spoke about at one of the recent FCA meetings. "What was that verse he quoted?" she thought. "Oh yeah. It was Mark 4:23, which states, 'If anyone has ears to hear, let him hear.'"

It then occurred to her that this principle works both ways, for good and for evil. Some of the same people who were so receptive to what she was saying suddenly seemed just as eager to stand with those attacking her. She then remembered another verse from the Bible that states, "A double-minded man is unstable in all his ways. Let not that man think he will receive anything from the Lord."

Charlotte then whispered under her breath. "There's a lot of double-minded students in this class."

# XIV.

Danny walked to his next period class still reveling in his recent triumph. He noticed Brock alone, looking for books in his locker.

"Why was Brock alone?" he thought. "He and Kent have always been inseparable, but it seems they have been spending more and more time apart lately."

He then thought this presented the ideal conditions to put his plan into action. He fully intended to lead Brock to the junkyard, release the mountain lion, and let nature run its course.

With Brock suddenly alone, there would be no one around to get in the way, he thought. He then projected commands toward Brock to follow him.

Brock sorted through his locker looking for his elusive biology book. "Where is that book? Why do I always have trouble keeping track of it?" he grumbled. Last week he scored a zero on an open-book biology quiz because he absent-mindedly left the book on his bed when he left for school.

Brock continued looking for the book when he suddenly felt himself feel tired as though something was draining his strength. In a daze, he looked up and saw Danny staring at him. "Oh hey, Danny. Do you need something?"

He suddenly had the urge to follow Danny. But why? A war was brewing in his mind, and he fought with all his strength to maintain control. He would take a few steps toward Danny and then stop. It was as if he were struggling between two paths; one determined by his own will, the other determined by another's. And the latter was gradually beginning to gain control.

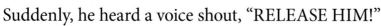

Suddenly, he heard a voice shout, "RELEASE HIM!"

He turned just long enough to see Johnny's face before he blacked out.

# XV.

Johnny was on his way to class when he realized he needed to talk to Brock. Brock had become his go-to person when it came to questions about football, and he had a question about a new play Coach Miller had introduced to the team the week before. As he walked toward Brock's locker, he suddenly had the strong sensation that Brock was in trouble. Brock's locker was out of view around the corner, but he knew that he knew something was wrong. He didn't know how he knew, but something inside of him made it clear that if he did not reach Brock's locker soon, something terrible would happen, so he began to jog.

As he turned the corner, he saw Brock on one knee, like he was struggling against something or someone. What made the scene even stranger was the image of his childhood friend brooding over Brock with a look that he could only be described as pure evil.

Johnny intended to ask Danny what was going on, but as he began to speak, he felt that familiar surge of power come over him, and from deep within, the words "RELEASE HIM" came out with an authority that shocked him.

Immediately, after speaking the words, he saw Brock collapse to the ground. He then found himself face-to-face with Danny. But this was not the same Danny he grew up with and knew. It was as if someone or something had taken over his friend. The look on his face dripped with hatred. For a moment, Johnny felt a tinge of fear. But as soon as it came, the power that came over him quenched it. The best way Johnny could describe it was the way a fire dies when it loses oxygen and fizzles out. He then calmly asked Danny what was going on. Instead of answering, Danny just stared at him with those disturbing pitch-black eyes. Johnny attempted to repeat his question, but before he could speak, a weariness came over him as though something was draining his strength. He then heard the same inner voice that had spoken to him before command him to resist. He knew it to be the same voice the way a person knows the voice of a friend, but this time the voice spoke with authority the way a commander commands his soldiers. Johnny then snapped himself out of his daze and, with a similar authority, turned suddenly toward Danny and shouted, "No!"

He then saw Danny stumble backward as though an invisible force crashed into him. The evil gaze that covered his face now seemed to be mixed with fear. The facial

expression of evil mingled with fear was an image Johnny would not soon forget. Danny then turned and ran toward the exit at the end of the hall and disappeared.

Johnny then turned toward Brock who still lay unconscious on the ground. After shaking him a few times, Brock slowly regained consciousness. When he awoke, he saw Johnny looking down at him, speaking words he had trouble making out. As the words became less and less garbled, he heard Johnny asking, "Are you okay?"

"Yes. I'm okay," replied Brock. "What happened?"

"I was going to ask you the same thing. I was coming to meet you at your locker when I saw you and Danny in what appeared to be a battle of wills."

"Oh yeah. Now I remember. I was going through my locker when I suddenly felt extremely nauseous. I turned around, and there was Danny, just staring at me with his beady black eyes. The next thing I knew, you're were kneeling next to me, asking if I was okay. Man, I feel like my head has been through a meat grinder. Where is Danny anyway? I feel like he had something to do with all this."

"He's not here. Do you need to go to the infirmary?"

"No. I'll be okay. Just let me sit here for a few to gather my wits. I'm glad you came along. I'm not sure what Danny was up to, but the look on his face had evil written all over it. I'm not a religious person, but I know evil when I see it."

# XVI.

Danny was several blocks away from the school when he realized he was still running. He wasn't sure why he was running. All he remembered was the fire in Johnny's eyes and the strong urge to flee from his presence. He slowed down to a walk and realized that his running had brought him to the junkyard where he was keeping the mountain lion. To his alarm, the cage was open, and the animal was nowhere in sight.

"Oh well. I'll just need to figure out another way to get back at Brock," Danny thought.

Danny proceeded to walk home. After nearly fifteen minutes of walking, Danny neared the entrance to his subdivision. As he walked, an ambulance sped by him toward the road where he lived. He didn't think much of it.

"Someone in the neighborhood must have an emergency," he thought.

When he reached the street where he lived, he noticed the ambulance had stopped near his home, where two police squad cars had also stopped. Alarmed, Danny began to jog toward home. He noticed several of his neighbors looking at him with sadness, with hands over their mouths. This caused even greater alarm, which turned his jog into a sprint. When he reached his home, he noticed a large animal lying dead on the front lawn

with a bullet wound in its chest. The scar on the animal's side identified it as the mountain lion he was keeping caged at the junkyard before it escaped.

The next sight caused Danny's heart to drop. There, lying on the front lawn, was his mother surrounded by several medics desperately trying to save her life.

Apparently, after escaping from the cage, the mountain lion made its way to the neighborhood and had attacked his mother who was doing yardwork at the time. A neighbor heard his mother's cries for help and mortally shot the animal. However, the animal was able to inflict terrible damage before it was shot, and his mother was now fighting for her life. Danny rushed to his mother's side and grabbed her hand. His mother looked up at him and, with tears rolling down her face, silently thanked the Lord for preserving her life so she could see her son one more time.

Danny knew instinctively that she was near death and that the only reason she was still holding on was because of him. She attempted to speak to him, but the words only came out in a whisper. In that moment, the love he had for his mother caused the apathy that had consumed him to disappear, and with tears streaming down his face, he leaned over so he could hear her. She then told him that she loved him before taking her final breath. Danny sat motionless by her side. How did this happen? How could this happen? He then realized this happened because of him. The realization hit him like a ton of bricks and caused a guttural moan to come out of him so painfully grief-stricken that it unsettled

everyone around. A policeman who stood by watching calmly walked next to Danny and lifted him. Danny then went limp into the officer's arms who half-carried him as he led him to the house.

# XVII.

A few months had passed since the incident, and life seemed to finally start coming back to normalcy for Danny. He had since moved in with his uncle, and the home he and his mother shared was sold at auction.

The confrontation Johnny had with Danny in the hallway involving Brock still weighed heavy on Johnny's mind, but something in him strongly wanted to go to Danny to console him after his mother's passing. Despite everything that had occurred, the years-long friendship he and Danny shared was hard to break. He made several attempts to approach Danny at school, but every time Danny would simply walk away.

One night Johnny had a dream where he, his mother, and Danny were sitting around a table, laughing and eating dinner together. He woke up and thought it strange that he would have such a dream. For months, Danny had given him the cold shoulder, and he could see no circumstance where such a dream could become reality. He then heard the same inner voice that spoke to him so often before say, "Invite Danny to live with you and your mother."

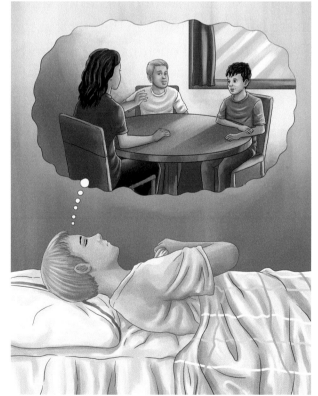

"Huh? Did I just hear that right? You want me to invite Danny to live with us?" Johnny thought.

Immediately, the inner voice replied, "Yes."

Johnny had learned over time not to ignore or dismiss that inner voice, so while eating breakfast, he brought the subject up with his mother. "Mom, I believe we are supposed to invite Danny to live with us."

Johnny expected his mother to say absolutely not. But to his surprise, his mother replied, "I was thinking the exact same thing." She continued, saying, "You and Danny have always been like brothers, and more than anything, Danny needs a brother in his life."

The next day Johnny decided he would not try to approach Danny at school. Instead, after school, he visited him at his uncle's home.

He knocked several times at the door, but no one answered. He began to leave when he heard the door open.

Danny opened the door, slowly at first and stopped opening when he recognized Johnny.

"What do you want, Johnny?" Danny asked.

"I just want to talk. Every time I try to speak to you at school, you seem to ignore me, so I thought I would have better luck if I came here."

For several seconds, Danny simply looked at Johnny through the crack in the door and said nothing. Then to Johnny's relief, Danny continued opening the door and said, "Come in."

Danny sat down at the kitchen table, and Johnny took this as his queue to do the same. Even after so many months, the deep pain of loss was etched all over Danny's face. Johnny had noticed glimpses of this while at school, but Danny had managed to cover up his grief while at school. But here at his uncle's home, he had let all his defenses down, and what Johnny saw was a broken person under the deep throes of despair.

He had heard of people who despaired of life. Johnny thought, "This is what it must look like."

A realization then hit Johnny like a ton of bricks. From their youth, he and Danny had been the closest of friends. When one seemed to be taken advantage of, the other always came to his defense. They had been

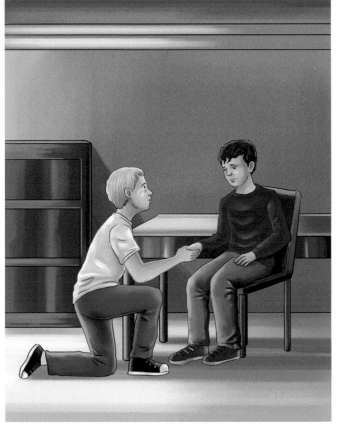

brothers in the truest sense, and nothing could separate them. It was as though God had brought them together because he knew they would need each other. But when Danny needed him the most, he was not there.

As Johnny sat there watching his friend, the tears came slowly at first. But they soon became a storm that overwhelmed him, developing into uncontrollable heaves.

Taken aback by Johnny's sudden emotions, Danny walked over to him. Johnny then fell to his knees and, while holding Danny's hand, said, "I'm sorry. I'm sorry. I'm sorry. I'm sorry. I'm sorry."

The sight of his friend's genuine pain broke something inside of Danny. Up to this point, he believed himself to be alone and an outcast for whom no one cared. But Johnny was proving this belief to be wrong. Before he knew it, both he and Johnny were crying in each other's arms.

# XVIII.

Johnny and Danny walked up to the address they had been given by a friend for that week's meeting. They knocked on the front door and was greeted by Charlotte.

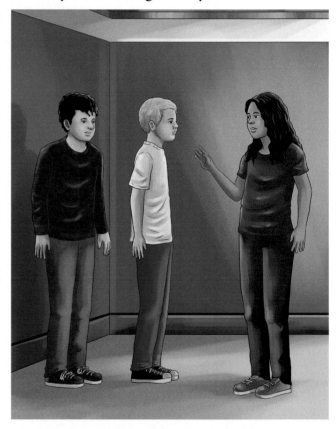

"Oh hey, Johnny. Thanks for coming. And who is your friend?"

"This is Danny. I believe you and him are in history class together," replied Johnny.

"Oh yeah. Now I remember you," stated Charlotte. "There's something different about you. I didn't realize you had blue eyes."

After the meeting, Johnny and Danny

walked home. When they walked in the house, their mom already had dinner set up. The boys ran to the table, eager to chow down on the steaming food.

"Slow down, boys," replied their mother. "There's enough to go around for everyone."

They then held hands as their mother prayed over the food.

As everyone ate and laughed at one another's jokes, Johnny never felt so fulfilled.

He then remembered the dream he had so many months before and how incredulous it  seemed at the time. He then understood how important it is to trust God and that the greatest fulfilment truly comes from obeying His instruction.

Printed in the United States
By Bookmasters